Tribute To A Village

Tribute To A Village

And Other Poems

Annette C. Sukarloo-Campbell

iUniverse, Inc.
New York Lincoln Shanghai

Tribute To A Village
And Other Poems

All Rights Reserved © 2004 by Annette C. Sukarloo-Campbell

No part of this book may be reproduced or transmitted in any form or by any means, graphic, electronic, or mechanical, including photocopying, recording, taping, or by any information storage retrieval system, without the written permission of the publisher.

iUniverse, Inc.

For information address:
iUniverse, Inc.
2021 Pine Lake Road, Suite 100
Lincoln, NE 68512
www.iuniverse.com

ISBN: 0-595-31698-0 (pbk)

ISBN: 0-595-77520-9 (cloth)

Printed in the United States of America

I dedicate this:

To the memory of my mother and father Annie & William F. Sukarloo, who did not wait long enough for this book to be published before they passed on, but who labored all their lives and made the memories of these poems possible for me.

To my husband, Antonio Campbell who waited a long time and supported me as I got my thoughts together.

To my five sisters and their husbands, my two brothers and their wives, who shared growing up with me and hope that I depicted some of their thoughts also.

To my nieces and nephews, who shared many memories with me and helped to fill in the blanks in my everyday life.

To all those people who have gone on ahead or are still with us who experienced life as it was and created the foundation for these poems.

To the many family and friends who came to my aid, loved me and supported me during the last days of my mother and father's illness.

To my friend Sher Elliott who for many years in her unique way helped me reclaim the spirited zest for life.

To my friend, Jessica R. Lee who made this publication possible with her encouragement and many acts of kindness.

To you dear reader. As you take this journey with me into the past and experience the joy and pain of life perhaps it will invoke some of your own memories and make up for my inadequacies.

Contents

PREFACE . . . . *xi*

I. HOME SWEET HOME 1
MOTHER WAITS FOR ME *3*
MORNING GLORY *5*
THE APPLE TREE *7*
THE SWING AND THE APPLE TREE *9*
SOME THINGS REMEMBERED *11*
HAPPY DAYS *13*
SUMMER DAYS *15*
PLAYTIME *17*
KITES *19*
RAINY DAY *21*
NIGHTTIME AT CARTREF *23*
EVENING TIME *25*
WASH DAY *27*
THE MASALA STONE *29*

II. EVERYDAY LIFE. 31
DRY DAYS *33*
EARLY MORNING BUS *35*
ONE WITH THE ROAD *37*
MARKET DAY *39*

THE TOWN CLOCK	43
THE POST OFFICE	45
SCHOOL TIME	47
THE NEIGHBOR'S SAVAGE	49
TRIP TO THE BEACH	51
UNANSWERED QUESTIONS	53
TIRED DEACON	55
VILLAGE SMELLS	57
VILLAGE SOUNDS	59
IDLERS	63
THE FENCE	65
HOLE DAWG	67
WHEN KATIE RAN AWAY	69
BEAUTY	71

III. SAYING GOODBYE 73

THE DREAD OF CHANGE	75
GOING HOME—GOODBYE TO MOTHER	77
JOY IN THE MORNING	79
TEN THOUSAND MEMORIES	81
HOPE FOR THE MORNING—GOODBYE FROM FATHER AND MOTHER	83
FATHER'S LEGACY	85
TRIBUTE TO A VILLAGE	87
RECESS LAMENT	91
SHOPKEEPER SALUTATION	95
FAREWELL TO THE WOODS	99
ADIEU TO YOUTH	101

GLOSSARY *103*
Index *107*

PREFACE

This is a collection of very personal poems depicting my humble experience from early childhood years through adulthood while living in the obscure village of Hopewell, St. Mary, Jamaica, West Indies.

My only qualification for writing these poems is that I am a second-generation village dweller and a first-hand witness. I lived with my parents and seven siblings who were among the first dwellers to bring life to a village that was in the making. The occupants who might never have been heard of before now lived a simple and unpretentious life. English was the first language but a local vernacular, Patois, was used as exemplified in, "Hole Dawg" which is an announcement that someone is at your gate and has come to visit you, so restrain your bad dog.

It took much motivation to start life from the very beginning without the comfort of established houses, shops, electricity, running water, paved roads, telephone or transportation. However, these difficulties only helped to create a group of people who were resilient, resourceful, innovative, modest, and wise in everyday living. The images of life back then will forever remain fresh in my memory: building a house from scratch; carrying water from the stream for everyday needs; mixing cement mortar to make blocks from a home-made wooden mold; being afraid of the thick darkness after sunset; experiencing the joy of morning; making friends with neighbors who were starting out life also; establishing life at work; making trips to the post office and attending school in the nearby town of Highgate; and walking miles to church which was in another town called Richmond. All these journeys were an attempt to have a worthwhile and balanced life.

The hardest experience of all was saying goodbye to my parents after 42 years of knowing them. "Joy In The Morning" portrays my cherished hope that I will see them again someday. There were many happy days and sad days, all of which made up the fabric of life. My only regret is that I procrastinated writing this book before the final days of my parents and some of my other family members. These poems tell somewhat of the relentless sprit of the dwellers, the privileged joys of being alive, the lament of the mortality of life, and the journey taken towards eternity as in a "Tribute To A Village."

HOME SWEET HOME

COMMON VILLAGE SAYINGS

"Disobedient pickney nyam rackstone."

Interpretation: Disobedient children will eat rock stone.

Meaning: Disobedient children will have a difficult life.

MOTHER WAITS FOR ME

I'm going back home where your fireside burns
    Filling my heart with gladness.
I'm going back home where the fireflies flicker
    And light up the starless nights.
I'm going back home where the crickets chirp
    And fill the stillness with music.
I'm going back home where your joy chases the darkness
    And soothes my fears.
I'm going back home where your laughter fills the valley
    And you always wait for me.

COMMON VILLAGE SAYINGS

"Wan wan coco full basket"

Interpretation: Coco collected one at a time will full the basket.

Meaning: Success takes time, it does not occur overnight

MORNING GLORY

Perched high on the logwood branch
The nightingale sings the morning chorus
And drives away the darkness of night.
Nature blinks and wipes slumber from her eyes.

Pink and orange clouds glow and hint that
The golden sun is on its way.
Gray shadows crayon the valley and
White mist cuddles the foot of the hills.

Honeybees stir among the tiny yellow
Logwood blossoms that softly fall to the earth.
Morning air dilutes pungent smoke rising
From the coal mound that smothered all night.

The sun lifts high above the bamboo grass
Which whine and crack against
Each other in the wind,
While shadows flee to escape the new day.

A bewildered owl sits on the mango branch
And blinks at sudden daylight.
He must wait for darkness while I hurry to sow
And harvest before shadows fall and no one can work.

COMMON VILLAGE SAYINGS

"Six a wan an haff a dozen a de adda."

Interpretation: Six of one and half a dozen of the other.

Meaning: Some things are equivalent to each other and it does not really matter which one you choose.

THE APPLE TREE

Your green waxen leaves
Shimmer in the sunlight
And catch shiny dewdrops
That sparkle like polished gems.
Your juicy red fruits and
Tender pink buds weigh heavily
Upon your drooping boughs.

I frolic among your branches
And my childish antics quickly
Disturb your delicate blossoms.
They loosen and fall
Like gentle rain wafting
On sighing breeze carpeting
The earth in pink finery.

Perhaps you silently weep
For your fallen blossoms,
Like a nursing mother
Weaning her suckling child,
Before he's forever gone from
The safety of the cradle and the breast.

COMMON VILLAGE SAYINGS

If yu can't ear den yu wi feel"

Interpretation: If you can't hear then you will feel.

Meaning: If you are disobedient then you must suffer the consequences.

THE SWING AND THE APPLE TREE

The rugged swing my brother
Made with sisal rope
And wooden seat
Hangs cautiously from
Your towering limbs.

From our tethered seat
My sister and I,
Above the highest pinnacle
Of the green banana grove,
Wistfully fly.

No one could stop us
From touching the clouds,
Except you.
Playfully you've often tossed us
From our lofty perch to the earth.

Humbly we'd sprawl
Like wet noodles upon the ground,
And after crying and laughing
Simultaneously,
We'd rise amid our pain to fly again.

COMMON VILLAGE SAYINGS

"Hass can't too good fe carry im own grass."

Interpretation: The horse can't be too good to carry his own grass.

Meaning: There should be no task considered low especially for the one who will benefit the most.

SOME THINGS REMEMBERED

The pleasure of finding the first ripe mango
    On the tree in the backyard.
Happily playing baseball with the neighbors
    On a Sunday afternoon.
Taking a refreshing bath in the nearby stream
    Leaving the fragrance of soap in the woods.
Listening to the heavy raindrops beating
    Like pebbles on the galvanized roof.

Feeling peaceful at sunset and watching
    The flicker of the kerosene lamp.
Waking up to the sound of the mourning doves
    As they heckle each other for attention.
Feeling the warmth of sunlight creeping
    Through the jalousie windows,
And smelling the aroma of chocolate and cinnamon
    Brewing on the fire.

COMMON VILLAGE SAYINGS

"Gimmi basket fe carry wata."

Translation: You give me basket to carry water.

Meaning: Someone is given an impossible task to do.

HAPPY DAYS

The joy of friends and relatives visiting
    To break the humdrum of life.
Eating special holiday meals
    With many loved ones on the verandah.
The pleasure of playing dominoes with father
    And watching him cheat with a straight face.
Having plenty of water in the barrels
    To last a long time.
Enjoying the smell of overseas in a
    Visiting relative's suitcase.
Anticipating a visitor after hearing the sound of a car
    From a distance creep along the pot-holed graveled road.
Listening to the church bells ring from far away
    And fill the air with music.
Watching the hummingbirds swiftly collect nectar
    From the garden at noontime.
Feeling peaceful to be home
    Where worries seem so far away.

COMMON VILLAGE SAYINGS

"Chicken merry hawk deh near."

Translation: When the chicken is merry the hawk is near.

Meaning: When things look too good to be true danger is near.

SUMMER DAYS

Summer brings joyful days
    Of school in weeks of recess.
There'll be sunny days when the
    Cool winds rush from the fields,
And ripened mangoes fall willing from the trees
    Making it easy for all to gather.

There will be days of roasting breadfruit
    And cod fish on open fires,
Drinking coconut water and sugarcane juice
    To cool our thirst from the sweltering heat.
Fetching water from nearby streams
    When the large metal barrels run dry.

There'll be days of making almond and coconut drops
    From the nuts gleaned in the fields.
There'll be time to beat chocolate beans
    With the iron pestle and wooden mortar.
Time to shell peas and thrash dandelion pods
    Dried by the sun.

There'll be no time for arithmetic calculations
    Or lessons from the grammar book.
That's too much knowledge for my dizzy head
    As I daydream of carefree days that beckon me.
So let me bask in the sunshine of summer days
    Filled with adventure that knows no end.

COMMON VILLAGE SAYINGS

"Wan yeye man a king ina bline country."

Interpretation: One-eyed man is king in the country of the blind.

Meaning: Things may not be as bad as they seem, there is always someone worse off than you.

PLAYTIME

There are many days of
Playing dolly-pot[1],
And pretend shopkeeper.
Make believe grocery stores
Stocked with empty cans of chocolate,
Sardine, corned beef, and milk.
Empty syrup and soft drink bottles
Stand neatly on plywood shelves.

Tiny yellow coconut buds collected
And wrapped up as brown rice
In sheets of old newspaper.
Make believe scale with cardboard hands
That don't move to weigh your goods.
Come buy corn for your wooden horse,
Perhaps he'll carry you
As you carried him.

---

1. A pretend game played to portray family life and household responsibilities.

COMMON VILLAGE SAYINGS

"Dawg sey if im have money im would buy im own flea."

Interpretation: The dog said if he had money he would buy his own fleas.

Meaning: Some folks who end up with unexpected money sometimes waste it on unnecessary things.

KITES

Come and watch my brother
Make his kites
From coconut bona[2] and
Brightly colored paper.
Frames held tightly together with twine
And homemade glue from the cedar tree.

Kites hoisted with long cloth tails
And flapping paper wings
Flying like hawks in the sky.
Kites casting eerie shadows on the ground
Frightening hens and baby chickens
Into running for a hiding place.

Kites attached to large balls of twine,
Tied to stubby guava pegs
Firmly hammered into the ground.
Kites flying high until summer winds die
And the sky grudgingly spits them out
Capsizing in dizziness to the ground.

---

2. The midrib of the coconut frond.

COMMON VILLAGE SAYINGS

"Rain a fall but de dutty tuff."

Interpretation: The rain is falling but the ground is still hard.

Meaning: When hard times hit sometimes nothing seems to help.

RAINY DAY

Be glad you're home on a rainy day
Not in the fields
Running for shelter
And hiding from the lightening.

There's much to do on a rainy day—
Mending socks that lost their dignity,
Polishing lampshades long neglected
Or writing that letter that is overdue.

When the rain comes in torrents
The wood shed is drenched,
Suffocating smoke rises from the fireside,
But meals taste better on a rainy day.

There'll be plenty of water
Caught in the metal barrels,
Plenty of mud scattered in the yard
Daring you to go outdoors.

So come rest awhile,
Read that storybook from the library,
And listen to the sounds
That only a rainy day brings.

COMMON VILLAGE SAYINGS

"Duppy no hu fe friten."

Interpretation: The ghost knows whom to frighten.

Meaning: There are some people who will pick on those who can't defend themselves.

NIGHTTIME AT CARTREF

Night has come too soon,
Playthings must be put away
And happiness must end,
For darkness brings suspicion.

Fear hears many voices;
The howling dog makes me sad –
It means someone will soon die.
Will it be my mother?

I stop my ears to end the madness,
For nighttime makes mother ill.
Her coughing and wheezing
Frighten me still.

The jukebox in the distant grocery shack
Plays the 60's tunes all night
And mixes with the haunting voices of the
Wrap-head women caught in ritual trance.

The mournful chants of the women
Dancing on the dark street corner
Drift in the wind up the hill
To my room where I lie in bed.

The fearful sounds lodge in my ears
And dreading the unknown makes me shiver.
So Lord I pray just one more time
Deliver us through another night.

COMMON VILLAGE SAYINGS

"Every dawg im day and puss im 4 a'clack."

Interpretation: Every dog has his day and the cat has his time (his 4 o'clock).

Meaning: Your day will come soon or later.

EVENING TIME

Evening shadows slowly creep across the sky
Like heavy curtains draping fragile windows.
Deliberate shadows knowing no haste
Giving time for all to settle in.

The chickens are first to say goodnight.
They climb the angled bamboo pole
Like a ladder to the cocoa tree to rest in safety
From ferocious dogs that prowl in the dark.

Clotheslines cleared and put away
And aluminum wash pans stored in the shed.
Drying trays of dandelion seeds and cocoa beans
Safely rescued from damp night air.

Wicks of kerosene lamps and lanterns
Trimmed and lit to drive away the darkness.
Then at bedtime wicks of lights put out
So all can sleep and restfully dream.

Doors and windows securely fastened,
While family dogs keep vigilant watch
From their shadowed lookout on the verandah
Until all are safely ushered into morning light.

COMMON VILLAGE SAYINGS

"Craven choke puppy."

Interpretation: Greed will choke the puppy.

Meaning: Don't bite off more than you can chew.

WASH DAY

Cold water gurgles and spills over
Rocks with slimy green moss.
Canopies of rose-apple trees and
Bamboo grasses block the sun.

It's washday and heavy load
Carried on laden head.
Bare feet touch chilling water
Recoiling.

Aluminum wash pan spills its load,
White foam rises and floats away.
Some garments fall to the bottom
Others try to escape with the flow.

Runaways retrieved with a guava staff,
Swishing, twisting
Paddling, wringing
Until all subdued.

Pale wrinkled fingers and tired hands,
Cold gray feet and laden head
Return to rusting wire lines
And winnowing breeze.

COMMON VILLAGE SAYINGS

"Scarnful dawg nyam dutty pudden."

Interpretation: The scornful dog eats dirty pudding.

Meaning: Don't be too scornful or finicky or else you might end up in a worse state than you started out in.

THE MASALA STONE

Remember the masala stone?
Heavy and flat
Sitting in the back yard?
Grinding onions, curry, pepper,
Tomatoes, and salt to a rich paste,
Flavoring every morsel
Remembered for a lifetime.

EVERYDAY LIFE

COMMON VILLAGE SAYINGS

"Nu broom sweep cleen but de ole wan no de cana."

Interpretation: The new broom sweeps clean but the old one knows the corners.

Meaning: The young person may be swift but age teaches wisdom and patience.

DRY DAYS

There'll be days when
>Water barrels are empty,
>Trickling streams run dry,
>The brown earth is parched,
>Dogs pant under the hibiscus hedge,
>And the pea leaves wither on the vine.

There'll be days when
>It's time to ardently pray for rain.
>So set up the large metal barrels,
>Put out the clay water pots,
>Come in quickly from the fields,
>And wait in faith for the blessing.

COMMON VILLAGE SAYINGS

"Yu neva se smoke widout fiah."

Interpretation: You'll never see smoke without fire.

Meaning: There is a reason for every action.

EARLY MORNING BUS

It's a long night to prepare for
The bus in the morning.
You must be up before the sun.
Your clothes laid out on the chair,
Bags packed and ready
Breakfast prepared and left overnight
Waiting to be eaten hot or cold.

The journey to catch the bus
Will take its toll.
You'll be tired before you get there.
Cat napping is best during the night,
You must listen for the clock alarm.
If you miss the bus in the morning
You'll wait for the one in the evening.

COMMON VILLAGE SAYINGS

"Wanti wanti can't getti an getti getti nuh want it."

Interpretation: Those who want it can't get it, but others get it and don't want it.

Meaning: Some people don't appreciate what they have while others wished they could have these same things.

ONE WITH THE ROAD

I pick my way around potholes
And shift my load from side to side.
It's raining and my face is wet
From blinding spray
But I'm compelled to keep on walking.

The smell of hot tar
Purposely rises to meet me
As bubbles burst on the black asphalt.
I must keep to the side of the road
And let the cars rush by.

The roads are never the same—
Graveled paths that crunch and slide,
White marl that coats my shoes,
Brown dust from the dirt road
And gray clay that sticks like glue.

The smell of the pasture or the pigpen.
The threat of rain or the chilly wind,
The heat of the midday sun or the asphalt,
The slipping and sliding,
All can make you mad.

Tired though I get
I must keep on walking,
For I have no transport but my feet,
The joy of the travel yet is mine
Because I'm one with the road.

COMMON VILLAGE SAYINGS

"Wa nuh kill fatten."

Interpretation: What won't kill you will fatten you.

Meaning: Don't be scornful of what is placed before you to eat. Enjoy it and be grateful for what you have received.

MARKET DAY

Higglers come in numbers large
Changing the stillness into a market place.
Last night only empty wooden stalls stood
Silently upon bare concrete floors.

Today life is full and vibrant sellers
Dipped in many decades of toil,
Flaunt goods arrayed in symmetry,
Beckon you to buy from every side.

The spice man smells like curry,
Sits on a wooden box with feet unclad.
His head draped in bright red
Mostly to bring him good luck.

Green scallions and callaloo[1] tied in bundles,
Yams, potatoes, and red peas exposed in open sacks.
Coconuts, mangoes, and oranges spread on linen bags
Display provisions in rich profusion.

Goods measured in pints,
Brimming over in metal cans.
Goods measured in pounds,
Tipping scales held high for all to see.

Higglers keep dulled pencils behind the ears,
Used in haste to calculate sales
On greasy brown paper bags
Before goods are wrapped in stale newspaper.

continued

---

1. Spinach-like vegetable

Buyers hurrying to catch over-laden buses,
Driven by sweaty impatient drivers
Accused of revving engines superfluously
And blowing horns intended to make you nervous.

Roofs of buses covered with crocus bags
Stuffed with goods piled high to the sky,
Anxious passengers crammed inside
Sharing space with grocery bags and squalling kids.

COMMON VILLAGE SAYINGS

"Wile de grass a gro de hass a stave."

Interpretation: While the grass is growing the horse is starving.

Meaning: If you neglect the small responsibilities of life then it might be too late to take care of the big responsibilities.

THE TOWN CLOCK

The four-sided monument
Holds the town clocks.
They stand at attention
In the roundabout.
Four clocks in all—
Facing east, west, north, and south—
None keeping the same time.

Squatters staring aimlessly
Leaning passively against the clock.
Buyers drifting back and forth,
Never stopping to question
The dissonance of time.
Hearts drunken with worry and care,
Caught in the illusions of life.

Time is a doomful reminder
That those who come
Must eventually go.
Weary shoppers wishing to rest transiently
Hoping perhaps never to return to drudgery.
I marvel at such madness
And lament my mortality.

COMMON VILLAGE SAYINGS

"Watch pat neva bwile."

Interpretation: If you watch the pot it will never boil.

Meaning: All things will come to those who wait patiently.

THE POST OFFICE

Mail stacked in wooden cubicles lettered A to Z.
Grated windows guarding the clerk behind the counter.
Perhaps you're 2nd or 3rd in line –
Never the 1st to call out your name.
Holler loud above the others
And the clerk is compelled to hear you.

Christmas time is joyful at the post office;
You may get a prized letter
Or a package from abroad
Holding money and sometimes clothes.
Perhaps you'll get a love letter
Folded in romantic shapes with a photo
of your beloved lovingly smiling.

So wait your turn patiently in line
And holler out your name.
Sometimes the unpredictable clerk
Sitting behind the grated window
May reward your deliberate persistence.
She may pull you the envied letter
From the guarded wooden cubicle.

COMMON VILLAGE SAYINGS

"De hia de monkey clime de more im expose."

Interpretation: The higher the monkey climbs the more he is exposed.

Meaning: The higher one climbs up the ladder of success his weakness becomes more visible to the public.

SCHOOL TIME

See the girls dressed in blue tunics
And white blouses neatly pressed.
Boys dressed in wrinkled shirts
And matching khaki shorts.
All sit at wooden desks and wooden chairs.
One large schoolroom
Separated by blackboards
With distinction marking each class.
Every one hears when you err with the timetable,
And snicker at the thrashing by the teacher
With the thick leather belt or wooden ruler.

Class recessed and joyful children frolic
In the school yard until the hand-bell rings–
All too soon.
More hours of math and reading
Until the hand bell rings again–
Not soon enough.
Then anxious children wildly rush
To open doors like cattle to the stile.
First out
First for freedom
Last for learning.

COMMON VILLAGE SAYINGS

"Run like wen tunda clap puss ina pear walk."

Interpretation: Run like when the thunder catches the cat in the avocado grove.

Meaning: Be careful that what you are doing is right because if you are caught red-handed you might have to run with the speed of lightening.

THE NEIGHBOR'S SAVAGE

There's one challenge
I wish I never had–
Trying to hide
From the neighbors' dog
As I pass the dreaded gate.

With stick in hand,
I hold my breath,
Walk on tiptoe,
Shrink behind the hibiscus hedge
Bending low like a drooping willow.

That savage always hears my footsteps,
And with pleasures of a demon
Chases as I holler and run away
From the creature's terrible barks
And horrible jaws.

COMMON VILLAGE SAYINGS

"Yu bred butta two side."

Interpretation: Your bread is buttered on both sides.

Meaning: You are very fortunate and have things coming too easy to you.

TRIP TO THE BEACH

No planning necessary
    Just come go with us,
      The more the better.
No special clothing
    Just something to swim in—
      An old T-shirt and shorts perhaps.
No transportation provided
    Just take the bus part way—
    Walk part way.
Swimming often makes you hungry,
    Take some hard-dough bread,
    And some fried fish too.
If you have no food at home
    Pick some oranges along the way
    But watch out for the barbwire fences.
Swim and frolic all day long
    But remember
    Know when to quit!
Start your journey home before twilight
    Else it will be a long, dark
    Scary walk home.

COMMON VILLAGE SAYINGS

"Wen breeze a blo Jancro fly fasta."

Interpretation: When the breeze is blowing the crow will fly faster.

Meaning: Sometimes people try to find excuses to carry out their intentions but trying to blame someone else for what they are doing.

UNANSWERED QUESTIONS

How did the ugly woman
    Find the handsome husband?

Where does the taxi driver find space
    In his cab to fit one more person?

How can the man with crippled feet
    Steal and quickly run away?

Why the neighbor cooks all day
    And never has food to eat?

How a man who doesn't work the fields
    Sells produce at the market?

Why the rich man pretends to be poor
    And lives in poverty?

Why the man who works a shilling borrows
    From the one who works a penny?

How can the teenage girl give birth
    Without expecting a baby?

These are curious questions from someone
    Who requires absolute answers.

COMMON VILLAGE SAYINGS

"Wen bag full it can't ben an wen it empty it can't tan up."

Interpretation: When the bag is full it can't bend and when it is too empty it can't stand up.

Meaning: Try to find the balance in life, if you eat too much you can't function well and if you are too hungry you also won't function well.

TIRED DEACON

Have you ever seen a tired deacon
      Sitting limply on the pulpit,
          Waiting for the sermon to be over?
Head bowed low to his chest,
      Jaw relaxed,
          Glasses falling from his face.
Children snickering,
      Teenagers poking each other
          Adults pretending not to see.
Tired deacon, lifeless he may appear
      Worked the fields all week,
          Walked miles to church.
Tired deacon arrived on time,
      Needs much rest
          Before he journeys home.

COMMON VILLAGE SAYINGS

"Cackroach nuh business ina fowl fite."

Interpretation: The cockroach should not have any business in the fight between fowls.

Meaning: Mind you own business and you'll stay out of arms way.

VILLAGE SMELLS

Some smells I can't forget:
> The intangible odor of Ackee and salfish cooking together,
> Vinegary Escovich fish frying with onions,
> The sultry air rising from the earth after the rain,
> Pungent jackfruit ripening on the back porch,
> A whiff of cocoa and cinnamon brewing over the fire,
> Acrid smoke ascending from the burning coal kiln,[2]
> The frowsy smell of the dogs after soaking in the rain,
> Sweet-scented roses in the garden at sunrise,
> And the balmy smell of sun-dried linen on the clothesline.

---

2. Green logs were lit and covered up with earth forming a large mound. After many days of burning coal would be produced which be used for cooking.

COMMON VILLAGE SAYINGS

"If yu bade pig im go strait bak ina de mud."

Interpretation: If you bathe a pig he will go right back into the mud.

Meaning: You can't clean up someone's life by changing his outward appearance; his heart will have to be changed first.

VILLAGE SOUNDS

Remember:
The grinding racket of the overloaded
    Trucks changing gears over the hill,
Hearing the cool winds pass through
    The banana grove at noontime,
Listening to the squeals of the neighbor's pigs
    Receiving their morning ration of food.

Remember:
The rumbling sound of approaching rain
    Roaring like a hungry lion,
Shouts from the tinker announcing himself
    Seeking work to solder holes in pots and pans,
Warning clucks of the watchful hen
    When the chicken hawk flies overhead.

Remember:
The wails from the neighbor's kids
    Being whipped while begging for reprieve.
Happy laughter from children playing in the stream
    Forgetting their errand to the grocery shop,
The boastful voice of the neighbor directing traffic–
    The one vehicle maneuvering a turn at his gate.

        continued

Remember:
The thunderous din of the river in spate
    Carrying oceans of water after heavy rains,
Frightening chants of the folks bewitched in ritual dance
    Around the five-spouted lantern during the dark,
The annoyance of buzzing mosquitoes with evil intentions
    Requiring blood to amuse their wanton pleasure.

COMMON VILLAGE SAYINGS

"Fiah deh a mus mus tail im tink a cool breeze."

Interpretation: Fire is at the mouse's tail and he thinks it is cool breeze.

Meaning: One who is heading for trouble sometimes is too ignorant to be aware of the danger he is in.

IDLERS

You'll find them resting on stoops
    Staring at others as they pass.
You'll find them loafing under grocery sheds
    Playing dominos on makeshift tables.

Sometimes they're sitting on bar stools chatting,
    Holding beer bottles and cans for hours.
You'll find them huddled under streetlights
    Long after dark when the street is empty.

You'll find them slothfully squatting on the ground
    Drawing figures in the dirt with their bony fingers.
Their idle words wasted in the air
    And passions consumed in frivolity.

They have no need to find a job
    They're content to be indolent.
You'll find them collapsed against the monuments
    Drunk from idleness requiring much sleep.

COMMON VILLAGE SAYINGS

"Lang cut bring swet but shart cut bring blud."

Interpretation: The long road might bring sweat, but the short cut may bring blood.

Meaning: Don't always look for the short cuts in life; sometimes they can prove detrimental.

THE FENCE

Cruel barbed wire fences,
Stretching across the fields
Trying to stop us from
Taking the short cut to town.
Those guard wires won't stop us!
Lift the top strand with one hand,
Hold the bottom strand with one foot,
Crawl through the fence.
Be careful!
Watch your head
     Your feet
     Your back!

COMMON VILLAGE SAYINGS

"Sarry fe maga dawg im tun roun bite yu."

Interpretation: If you feel sorry for the starving dog he will turn around and bite you.

Meaning: Sometimes the one that you help might be ungrateful and try to harm you.

HOLE DAWG

Hole Dawg!
Miss Henny,
Anybody deh home?
A who dat?
A mi Miss Henny!
A hoe, a yu man!
Come in nuh.
Dawg gweh!
Go lay dung a bush
An' mek Mass Johnny come in.
Me glad fe se yu man!

COMMON VILLAGE SAYINGS

"Silent riva run deep."

Interpretation: Silent river runs deep.

Meaning: Be careful! Don't take people for granted.

WHEN KATIE RAN AWAY

Remember little Katie
Standing shy at the gate?
Her hands tightly folded,
Timid eyes cast to the ground
Hardly ever looking at you.

Shy little Katie
Her words were few.
If you'd talk to her
You'd get a giggle or two,
Her teeth showing from afar.

She kept her work in tune—
The sweeping, the cleaning,
The cooking and the reaping,
And fetching of water too
Without a willful grumble.

Then one day when the star-apples
Hung mellow upon the trees,
When the bananas were fit
And ready for the wharf,
Katie was not around.

You may never guess it—
Katie left without a word,
Gone forever from home.
Shy little Katie
Found herself a man.

COMMON VILLAGE SAYINGS

"Se mi an cum live wid mi a two diffrant tings."

Interpretation: To see me and come to live with me are two different things.

Meaning: You can't judge a book by its cover.

BEAUTY

Beauty was a donkey,
And she was bright.
She loved the children
Especially when they did right.

One day the children thought up a foolish thing
Not knowing what upon themselves they'd bring.
The two silly kids tried to force a ride
With heads filled with folly and pride.

Upon her back they both stupidly climbed
Without holding on they idly reclined.
Beauty bolted off in a sudden dash,
She was as quick as they were rash.

As fast as lightening she quickly flew
Down yonder where prickles thickest grew.
The senseless children wailed and fell like bricks
But Beauty spared them their well-earned kicks.

COMMON VILLAGE SAYINGS

"Haad aise mek saaf battam."

Interpretation: Hard ears make a soft bottom.

Meaning: If you can't comply with instructions then you will feel the pains of folly.

SAYING GOODBYE

COMMON VILLAGE SAYINGS

"Yu nuh no wat a'clack a strike."

Interpretation: If you only knew what hour the clock is striking.

Meaning Be aware of the times and happenings around you.

THE DREAD OF CHANGE

Today I visited my childhood home
And stood alone within its empty walls.
I thought I heard footsteps in the hallway,
Laughter from the flower garden,
Someone clearly calling my name,
But that could be only memories of long ago.

The cold slender fingers of the wind
Softly tapped upon the windowpane,
Sent shivers through the orange grove
And whispered to me the secret
It knew so long ago
That I was not willing to accept.

I now know its doleful secret,
And I'm beginning to understand
But I'm hardly comforted.
All things that exist must come to an end
And I should acquiesce
To change and rebirth.

COMMON VILLAGE SAYINGS

"Every day yu carry bucket go a well wan day de battam mus drap out."

Interpretation: If you carry the bucket to the well every day then one day the bottom will fall out.

Meaning: Always cherish what you have and don't take things for granted that it will always be available to you.

GOING HOME — GOODBYE TO MOTHER

Mother you told me you're going home,
I listen and watch with sadness
As you begin your journey without me.
But where is home?
Is it where the bougainvilleas bloom
And brighten the day,
Where the nightingale sings endlessly?
Is it where naseberries ripen
In the sweet month of April,
The month of your birth?

Do you know the way?
Shall I not go with you,
And end this night of weeping?
Is it beyond the blue skies,
Far away from sadness and pain?
Is it where death cannot enter,
And time has no power there?
Is it where my Lord lives?
And where eternity goes on forever?
Is it there, is it there sweet Mother?

COMMON VILLAGE SAYINGS

"Every hoe ave im tick a bush."

Interpretation: Every hoe has its stick in the bushes.

Meaning: There is someone out there suitable for everyone.

JOY IN THE MORNING

The cold earth now silently
Holds you within its passive breast.
No longer will I hear your voice
Nor feel your touch.
No longer can you see me
or converse with me.

Often I visit you in my dreams
Where we'd go on journeys together,
Pondering the things we've shared
Re-living the past,
The present,
But never the future.

You're at peace as you peacefully sleep
And wait for morning light,
When we'll again go on journeys together,
Not in the past,
Not in the present,
But into the future.

COMMON VILLAGE SAYINGS

"Ole fiah tick easy fe ketch."

Interpretation: The old firewood is easy to catch fire.

Meaning: If you obtained something and lost it, then it becomes easier to acquire it the second time round. This often refers to the love relationship between a man and a woman.

TEN THOUSAND MEMORIES

Ten thousand memories
> Remind us that you were here
> Faithfully loving us to the end.

Ten thousand days with you
> Slipped away in one fleeting moment
> Like the wick of the lamp blown out at night.

You'll forever dwell in our hearts,
> Renewing us with courage and love
> Just as you did ten thousand times before.

COMMON VILLAGE SAYINGS

"Anancy sey dat tree trubble betta dan wan."

Interpretation: The spider says that three troubles are better than one.

Meaning: Sometimes misfortunes don't come singly and it might be better to deal with many troubles all at once than having to go through them one at a time.

HOPE FOR THE MORNING — GOODBYE FROM FATHER AND MOTHER

We know you grieve for us but
We're free from pain and worry.
God saw it best to lay us down to rest.
It was hard when we left,
We know you wanted one more day
Just to hear our voice, feel our touch,
That's all we wanted too
But we had to go.

Things left undone must stay that way,
For the Master called us
And we had to go.
Don't burden your days with grief and pain,
Remember how we lived with you,
Not just when we said good-bye,
For we know for certain
We'll see you in the morning.

COMMON VILLAGE SAYINGS

"If yu can't ketch Quaw-Cu yu ketch im shut."

Interpretation: If you cant' catch "someone" then you can catch his shirt.

Meaning: If someone tries to harm you and he can't catch you then he might go after whatever he can get whether it's your goods or your family.

FATHER'S LEGACY

You didn't say much
But there's much to say about you,
The meekest one among us.
You could put sad days behind you
With a whistle or a smile.

Your dry humor will be remembered
And your jokes were harmless and amusing.
Your youthful tricks made us laugh.
You could win or lose a game
And pretend they were both the same.

You loved life but didn't say much,
You loved us but didn't tell us so,
You quietly left us without a goodbye,
But left behind a legacy–
The meekest one among us.

COMMON VILLAGE SAYINGS

"Danky sey de worle nuh level."

Interpretation: The donkey said that the world is not level.

Meaning: Life is not equal for all people.

TRIBUTE TO A VILLAGE

Today I said goodbye to a village,
Their occupants finally rest
As their toilsome journeys
Came to an end—one at a time
And all seem to be forgotten.

There's no laughter from children
Playing baseball on a Sunday afternoon.
No whistling from the fruitful fields,
No anxious waiting on the front veranda
For loved ones to arrive.

The sight of linen flopping on the
Clothesline has disappeared.
Harvesting bananas for the wharf
Has come to a sudden halt
And packing sheds are empty.

As night covers the lonely valley,
There's none to light the oil lamps.
At daybreak no smoke or smell of
Kerosene ascends from the fireside.
All that remains is cold gray ashes.

Family gatherings have become delusive
And holidays now have lost their meaning.
There's none to smile and welcome you,
There's none to feel heartache or pain
Or reminisce happy memories with you.

                continued

I can hear the mourning doves cooing
As I hurry away in a solitary procession
To escape the pain of a haunting silence,
While tenaciously guarding the memories
Of a village I knew so well.

COMMON VILLAGE SAYINGS

"De fus wata hag se im wash imself."

Interpretation: The first water the hog sees he will wash himself.

Meaning: Be sure to make use of opportunities when they first come your way.

RECESS LAMENT

Recess makes my heart glad and gives rest
From calculating sums[1] all day long.
I like to play stick-in-the middle[2]
And dodge the flying ball thrown at me
Or skip rope until my shoes fall off.
I love to sit under the spreading branches
Of the Poinciana tree and let my friend
Braid my hair then tie it with rubber bands.
Sometimes we'd play cockfight[3] with the delicate flowers
And mangle the red and yellow petals of the tree.

Children clapping hands and singing the merry tune of
"Farmer-in-de-dell," while dancing around the ring;
I'll be happy if I get picked even to be the cheese.
If I have a penny saved from yesterday
I'd run to the snow-cone man who is always waiting.
His wooden pushcart sits steady on homemade wheels.
He shaves a block of ice and puts it cold in my hands,
Then pours sweet red strawberry syrup on top.
The annoying bees that swarm the dripping syrup bottles
try to lick my snow cone as I squirm and run away.

continued

---

1. Arithmetic problems.
2. A game played with ball thrown intentionally to hit a person who is trying to dodge it.
3. A game played with parts of a flower between two people.

Schoolyard filled with noisy boys and girls
Dressed in sweaty uniforms
Coloring the yard in blue and white.
Children running, laughing, and playing joyfully.
This moment is a pause between their tiny worlds:
One of painful classroom lessons,
The other of household chores that have no end.
Children living for the frivolous moment;
Tomorrow seems so far away
And is not promised for those who play today.

COMMON VILLAGE SAYINGS

"If yu put im name pan bulla im nyam it."

Interpretation: If you wrote his name on the cake he will eat it without knowing what is written on it.

Meaning: Someone who is illiterate or too ignorant might not know what is at stake for him.

SHOPKEEPER SALUTATION

Shopkeeper, Shopkeeper,
Do you have what I want today?
Or should I walk a little further?
I will come in after I say how-do-you-do,
Maybe you'll be pleased to help me then.

I see your aerated water bottles
Neatly lined upon the shelves.
Flavored water with names like
Champagne, cream soda, and ginger beer
All that makes me thirsty.

Sir, do you have the red herring
And the best piece of salt-fish[4]
Hidden under the counter?
The pickled mackerel, the corned beef
And the pigs tail soaking in brine?

Is your scale hanging from the ceiling
And won't cheat the weight of things I want?
Let me have a pound of brown sugar, white rice,
Chicken-back, some salt, and flour too?
It's getting late so please help me soon.

                continued

---

4. Dried and salted codfish.

Your glass case shows the things I like,
Crackers, bulla[5] and cheese.
The flaw-flaw[6] of every kind looks so good.
Can I have some coconut drops,
Sweet potato pone, grater cake,
And some gizzadas[7] too?

---

5. Round, flat, cake-like pastry.
6. Homemade pastry of many kinds.
7. Pastry made with shredded coconut.

COMMON VILLAGE SAYINGS

"Bush ave aise an tree ave yeye."

Interpretation: The bush has ears and the trees have eyes.

Meaning: Be careful what you say it might come back to haunt you.

FAREWELL TO THE WOODS

At noon I visited the woods just one more time
    Seeking to find again that peace so sublime.
I tiptoed passed the hornets' nest
    Since I did not like them—even at their best.
I lingered long by the little brook,
    And of the watercress I partook.
I willfully disturbed the shy tadpoles
    That hid under the floating leaves—poor souls.
The pink orchids bid me gather blooms and waved to me
    From the shadowed boughs of the guango tree.
The soft green moss pillowed my staggering steps as I slipped
    Upon the hillside that curved and dipped.
I heard the Nightingale sang a song of sadness as I bade farewell
    For he knows a hundred reasons I would like with him to dwell.

COMMON VILLAGE SAYINGS

"Hag pickney sey mumma how yu mout so lang?"

Interpretation: The piglet said to his mother,
"Mother why is your mouth so long?"

Meaning: There are questions in life that can't be explained to children until they grow up and see for themselves.

ADIEU TO YOUTH

At morn I came riding through the woods
    With vitality.
My jet-black hair shone
    And glistened in the sunlight.
I climbed the mountains with vigor
    And ran the valleys with youthful glee.

At noon I blossomed in splendor
    And flourished in the summer rain.
I laughed in joyful tones
    And the hills echoed back my mirth.
Aches and pains I knew not of,
    And my feet glided with agility.

At twilight the damp dew fell
    Softly upon my brow,
The strength of my youth slowly faded
    And my radiance paled beneath the shadows.
To my demise I had lost the things I dearly cherished
    That I thought I held for eternity.

GLOSSARY

This is an inadequate endeavor to list and spell, and explain a few of the Jamaican words used throughout this book. The Jamaican dialect was orally passed down from generation to generation for many centuries. Most of the words can be pronounced and spelled differently from one parish to another in the island. Frequently many of the words do not have an exact translation. Sometimes words are duplicated for emphasis for example: "wan wan," is used to say that one of a particular thing is collected upon another; or if someone describes another person as, "fool-fool," it means that he is doubly stupid. The dialect was generated from many languages, which included English, French, Spanish, German, and many African languages.

A	am, is, it is.
aise.	ears
Anancey.	proverbial wise and witty spider
bade.	bathe
bak.	back
batam.	bottom
bline.	blind
blo.	Blow
blud.	blood
bred.	bread
butta.	butter
bwile.	boil
cana.	corner

clime.	climb
craven.	greedy
cum.	come
cuss.	curse
dat.	that
dawg.	dog
den.	then
dutty.	earth, soil, dirty.
dung.	down
drap.	drop
duppy.	ghost
edda.	other
fe.	for
fritten.	frighten
fiah.	fire
getti.	get it
fus.	first
gi.	give
gweh.	go away
gro.	grow
grung.	ground
haad.	hard
haff.	half
hag.	hog or pig
hass.	horse, stupid
hia.	higher
higgler.	peddler, seller in the market or street

hole.	old or whole
im.	him
ina.	into
jancro.	crow or vulture
ketch.	catch
lang.	long
maga,	meager, malnourished
man.	Endearing term for example: friend, honey
mass.	Mr. or sir.
masta.	master
mek.	make
mi.	me
mout.	mouth
mumma.	mother
mus.	must
mus mus.	mouse or mice
nyam.	eat
nuh.	no or not
pickney.	children
puss.	cat
Quaw-cu.	proverbial sly or cunning person
riva.	river
roun.	round
saff.	soft
sarry.	sorry
shaat.	short
sey.	say

suppa.	supper
ting.	thing
tink.	think
tuff.	tough
tun.	turn
*tund*a.	thunder
wan.	one
wanti.	want it
wata.	water
wid.	with
widout.	without
wi.	will
wile.	while, wild
worle.	world
yeye.	eye
yu.	you

Index

A
Anancy sey dat tree trubble betta dan wan 82

B
Bush ave aise an tree ave yeye 98

C
Cackroach nuh business ina fowl fite 56
Chicken merry hawk pick deh near 14
Craven choke puppy 26

D
Dankey sey de worle nuh level 86
Dawg sey if im have money im would buy im own flea 18
De fus wata hag see im wash imself 90
De hia de monkey clime de more im expose 46
Disobedient pickney nyam rackstone 2
Duppy no hu fe friten 22

E
Every dawg im day and puss im 4 o' clack 24
Every day yu carry bucket go a well wan day de battam mus drap out 76
Every hoe av im tick a bush 78

F
Fiah deh a mus mus tail im tink a cool breeze 62

G
Gimmi basket fe carry wata 12

H
Haad aise mek saff battam 72
Hag pickney sey mumma how yu mout so lang 100
Hass can't too good fe carry im own grass 10

I
If yu bade pig im go strait bak ina de mud 58
If yu can't hear den yu wi feel 8
If yu can't ketch Quaw-Cu yu ketch im shut 84
If yu put im name pan bulla im naym it 94

L
Lang cut bring sweat but shaat cut bring blud 64

N
Nu broom sweep cleen but de ole wan no de cana 32

O
Ole fiah tick easy fe ketch 80

R
Rain a fall but de dutty tuff 20
Run like wen tunda clap puss ina pear walk 48

S

Sarry fe maga dawg im tun roun bite yu 66
Scarnful dawg nyam dutty pudden 28
Se mi and cum live wid mi a two dirrerant tings 70
Silent riva run deep 68
Six a wan an haff dozen a de adda 6

W

Wa nuh kill fatten 38
Wan wan coco full basket 4
Wan yeye man a king ina bline country 16

Wanti wanti can't getti an getti geti nuh want it 36
Watch pat neva bwile 44
Wen bag full it can't ben an wen it empty it can't tan up 54
Wen breeze a blo Janco fly fasta 52
Wile de grass a gro de hass a stave 42

Y

Yu bred butta two side 50
Yu neva se smoke widout fiah 34
Yu nuh no wat a'clack a strike 74

PERSONAL NOTES

PERSONAL NOTES

PERSONAL NOTES

PERSONAL NOTES

0-595-77520-9

Printed in the United States
21532LVS00001B/88-105